MARY AND THE
CATHOLIC IMAGINATION

MARY AND THE CATHOLIC IMAGINATION

Le Point Vierge

WENDY M. WRIGHT

**2010 Madeleva Lecture
in Spirituality**

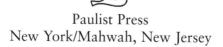

Paulist Press
New York/Mahwah, New Jersey

Book and cover design by Lynn Else

Library of Congress Cataloging-in-Publication Data

Wright, Wendy M.
   Mary and the Catholic imagination : le point vierge / Wendy M. Wright.
      p. cm. — (Madeleva lecture in spirituality ; 2010)
   Includes bibliographical references (p.   ).
   ISBN 978-0-8091-4707-6 (alk. paper)
      1. Mary, Blessed Virgin, Saint—Devotion to—California—Los Angeles Region. 2. Los Angeles Region (Calif.)—Religious life and customs. 3. Catholic Church. Archdiocese of Los Angeles (Calif.) 4. Imagination—Religious aspects—Catholic Church. I. Title.
   BT652.U6W46 2011
   232.91—dc22

                                                      2010052060

Published by Paulist Press
997 Macarthur Boulevard
Mahwah, New Jersey 07430

www.paulistpress.com

Printed and bound in the
United States of America

Catholic Imagination MARY AND THE CATHOLIC
IMAGINATION **Mary and the Catholic Imagi-**
nation Mary and the Catholic Imagination MARY
AND THE CATHOLIC IMAGINATION **Mary and**
the Catholic Imagination Mary and the
Catholic Imagination MARY AND THE CATHOLIC
IMAGINATION **Mary and the Catholic Imagi-**
nation Mary and the Catholic Imagination MARY
AND THE CATHOLIC IMAGINATION **Mary and**
the Catholic Imagination Mary and the
Catholic Imagination MARY AND THE CATHOLIC
IMAGINATION **Mary and the Catholic Imagi-**
nation Mary and the Catholic Imagination MARY
AND THE CATHOLIC IMAGINATION **Mary and**
the Catholic Imagination Mary and the
Catholic Imagination MARY AND THE CATHOLIC
IMAGINATION **Mary and the Catholic Imagi-**
nation Mary and the Catholic Imagination MARY
AND THE CATHOLIC IMAGINATION **Mary and**
the Catholic Imagination Mary and the
Catholic Imagination MARY AND THE CATHOLIC
IMAGINATION **Mary and the Catholic Imagi-**
nation Mary and the Catholic Imagination MARY
AND THE CATHOLIC IMAGINATION **Mary and**
the Catholic Imagination Mary and the
Catholic Imagination MARY AND THE CATHOLIC
IMAGINATION **Mary and the Catholic Imagi-**

CONTENTS

Wendy M. Wright is professor of theology at Creighton University and holds the John C. Kenefick Faculty Chair in the Humanities. She also teaches regularly in several graduate ministerial programs including Creighton's Christian spirituality master's program and the National Methodist Academy for Spiritual Formation. With Dr. J. O'Keefe she is cohost of the Creighton University podcast "Catholic Comments." Dr. Wright holds a PhD from the University of California at Santa Barbara and teaches and writes in the areas of history of spirituality, family spirituality, spiritual direction, and the Catholic devotional tradition. She has written extensively about the Salesian spiritual tradition, and among her many publications is *Francis de Sales and Jane de Chantal: Letters of Spiritual Direction* in the Paulist Press Classics of Western Spirituality series.

INTRODUCTION

This particular exploration of the figure of the Virgin Mary and the Catholic imagination grows out of a larger research project that has occupied me for the better part of the past six years and that, in the course of time, I have come to understand as a pilgrimage. The pilgrimage road itself threaded through the car-clogged landscape of the Archdiocese of Los Angeles at whose center is America's "minority majority city," which is also my hometown and a microcosm of the global Catholic Church. The road led in the direction of what I have come to call "the story of Mary in L.A."[1] My pilgrimage journey led me to parishes and shrines—the "inns" at which I stopped—to interpretive guides provided by scholarly confreres, to fellow pilgrims who shared with me their tales, to my "relics": the photos, holy cards, and archival treasures that I collected along the way.[2] Through these I encountered the fascinatingly polymorphous religious symbol and touchingly intimate presence who answers to the name Mary. The pilgrimage put me in conversation with Catholics at all ends of the theological spectrum and from diverse cultural backgrounds and plunged me into the intensely performative milieu of devotional piety. Although I might have looked for her in any American city, Los Angeles was a particularly apt place to go in search of her. The sprawling, humming, magnificent, and tawdry urban environment on the west coast of California is not, strictly speaking, the City of the Angels. By official founding proclamation, it is *el pueblo de la Reyna de los Angeles*—the village of the Queen of the Angels. Actually, for decades historians and chroniclers have waffled back and forth between several possible original names, but whatever the historical accuracy of the matter, all the names include her. It is indisputably true that the city is Mary's. The angels may have come to stand in for her in common discourse, mine included, but this does not negate the fact that the city belongs to her. Nor does the name alone identify it as such; there she is palpably present and has been from the beginning.[3]

In the global Catholic environment of Los Angeles, the Virgin Mary takes many forms. She is encountered as the young woman spoken of in scripture and as the Madonna of legend. She appears as the ancient Byzantine *Theotokos* and is described by her early modern Litany of Loreto appellations such as Mystical Rose, Ark of the Covenant, and Tower of David. She is a regal presence and a humble sister, an apocalyptic warrior defending the faith and a peacemaker reconciling enemies. Her guises include the *virgenes* of Mexico—among them *Nuestras*

2

Señoras de Guadalupe, Juaquila, and *San Juan de los Lagos*—the Salvadoran *Nuestra Señora de la Paz* and *Nuestra Señora de Suyapa* of Honduras. I have encountered her as Vietnam's Our Lady of La Vang, as *Caridad* of Cuba, and Peñafrancia and Manaoag of the Philippines. She reigns among the martyred Armenians, as Poland's Black Madonna of Częstochowa, and as Queen of Lebanon, Lithuania, and Africa. Her dogmatic identities reveal her as the Immaculate Conception and the Assumption. In her city she displays her Immaculate Heart, inclines to her devotees as Mother of Grace and Good Counsel, and promises them succor as Our Lady of Perpetual Help. As Dolores and Soledad she is heavy with sorrows, and through the Rosary she celebrates her joys. Her people report her appearances at Lourdes, Mount Carmel, Knock, Tepayac, and Fatima (as well as in the Mojave desert) and commend her as miracle worker, intercessor, patroness of communities, guardian of nations, boundary keeper, the one who shelters all, the friend of the poor, and patron of the powerful. She belongs to all the people of the Los Angeles region no matter where they might be located on the theological, cultural, and ideological spectrum of American Catholic life.

As I have passed along my Los Angeles pilgrim road, I have seen that Mary occupies a richly textured, imaginative space in the wider Catholic imagination. She quite literally occupies large swaths of material and temporal space. But more strikingly,

3

she occupies a generous space in the hearts of those who speak to, look to, identify with, implore, honor, and hope in her. In a conceptual world in which sacred presence is powerfully sensed, she is among those presences most poignantly and deeply felt. This present essay grows out of that pilgrimage saga, which, in turn, has led me to reflect on the nature of the Catholic imagination as viewed through the figure of Mary and to suggest that she might be considered the global Catholic Church's *point vierge*. I will also suggest that the provocative phrase *le point vierge* is one that opens up a dimension of both the Catholic imagination and the mystery of Mary in an intriguing manner.

I am certainly not the first contemporary scholar to concern myself with Mary or to go on pilgrimage with the hope of encountering her. Feminist theologians Elizabeth Johnson and Sally Cunneen have dethroned and searched for her as a sister, Marina Warner criticized her for being "alone of all her sex," Chicana theologian Norma Alcarón alerted us to the oppressive culture of "Marianismo," Charlene Spretnak missed her and tried to redeem her traditional titles from the perspective of emerging scientific cosmology. British theologians Tina Beattie and Sarah Jane Boss have peered at her through the lens of French feminist philosophy and interdisciplinary studies. English cultural historian Ruth Harris went to the waters of Lourdes in search of a cure, while Harris's American counterparts

Paula Kane and Ann Matter have considered her apocalyptic identity and shed light on her "tabloid cult." Cultural anthropologist Sandra Zimdars-Swartz has scrutinized her apparitions, and William Christian Jr., Miri Rubin, and Linda Hall have chronicled her complex history. Art historians and those who study religious material culture have held up her multiform "old" and "new" world guises, and more academics than I can name here, Timothy Matovina, Virgil Elizondo, and Thomas Tweed in the forefront, have studied her sociological and cultural implications, especially for the ethnic communities that claim her.

All these intrepid explorers have undertaken their journeys, whether they consult them frequently or not, with guidebooks collated from generations of Catholic theological, conciliar, dogmatic, and contemplative reflections on the Virgin Mother of God.[4] These contemporary and historic fellow travelers have helped me inestimably to make sense of my topic. But in the final analysis it is Mary's devotees, those women and men in the archdiocese under her patronage with whom I have spoken and prayed, who have been my best teachers. As a scholar who concerns herself with "spirituality," I align myself most closely with "lived experience," especially the experience of persons who struggle to live out of the part of themselves that yearns for ultimacy and who are shaped and changed in the process.[5]

THE CATHOLIC IMAGINATION IN A MARIAN MODE

That there is such a thing as a "Catholic imagination" is the first assumption of this present exploration. Other scholars have written, more persuasively than I, of the existence of a perspective, a lens as it were, through which individuals steeped in the religious world of Roman Catholicism tend to approach the world.[6] Of what that imagination might consist is generally agreed upon, if variously nuanced. In my own fairly straightforward manner, I have come to understand it in this way. First, what is the imagination? In ordinary use the imagination tends to be equated with fantasy or science fiction. It suggests that which is *not* real. Alternately, the imagination might be seen as a peripheral capacity that some people happen to have in greater share than others. Artists, musicians—these people, it is said, have imagination. In contrast to this limited view, I side with contemporary philosopher Mary Warnock, who defines the imagination as a central human capacity that is crucial to perception itself.[7] In her view we do not directly perceive something called "reality"; rather, perception and interpretation occur simultaneously. We image, sort, organize, and see patterns and meaning at every moment. We need our imaginations, Warnock contends, to see what is familiar. We also need them to see what is *unfamiliar*. In addition, the very same capacity of imagining is utilized when we interpret patterns *beyond* what we directly perceive. We use the imagination to perceive the depth and nuance present in our world. Further still, we need the imagination to conceive the world *as it is not yet*. It is never enough for human beings to simply survive—to eat, reproduce, and protect ourselves. We are hungry for meaning. We must dream. We must build physical and mental universes of wondrous invention. We must fashion things of beauty. We must be sensitive to the brush of spirit, to hear the whisper of mercy, and conceive of justice in a world where it does not exist. What we dream, what we imagine, is not fantasy but depth, completion, and fulfillment. It is the work of the imagination at one and the same time to see what is familiar, to understand what is unfamiliar, to conceive of the new and the as yet unrealized, and to search out the ultimate depth and fullness of all that is.

A corollary of this is that different individuals and, especially, different communities possess distinctive imaginative lenses through which they perceive and evaluate their worlds and through which they register the longed-for hope of the human heart. Roman Catholicism is one of these communities. It certainly shares family features with other religious imaginative worlds, and its perspective is emphatically not monolithic. In fact, as I have made my way along my pilgrim road, I have been made deeply aware of the extent to which the Catholic Church has many adherents, many of whom live in very different cultural, ideological, linguistic, and aesthetic worlds. My pilgrimage has taken me, a progressive postVatican II American, into the luxurious environment of devotional Catholicism, which has required me to rethink the church to which I belong. Yet the Catholic imagination reflected there is finally a familiar one. It does, I and others with me insist, have certain features that are identifiable. Drawing upon the thought of an interdisciplinary band of scholars I will mention as well as upon my own insights, I will suggest that the polyvalent figure of Mary, as she manifests herself across the globe and through the centuries and finally arrives in the minority majority city of Los Angeles, both illustrates the distinctive Catholic imagination and finds in that imagination not the detritus of stasis or rigidity but the lively, if dormant, seeds of creativity, reconciliation, renewal, and hope. Mid-twentieth-century Jesuit literary scholar William Lynch wrote these challenging, even startling, words: "The primary goal of human life is the liberation of the imagination."[8] I'd like to take him up on the challenge and to at least contribute to the ongoing conversation about Mary and the role she plays in the imaginative life of contemporary Catholicism, a role I have come to describe as *le point vierge*.

If I might suggest some axial dimensions of such an imaginative world, I would say that, first, the Catholic imagination is profoundly sacramental. Andrew Greeley described it as an "enchanted imagination." Put simply, the Catholic imagination tends to be open to the possibility of space and time opening out into the infinite and eternal as well as open to the possibility that the created world by analogy gives expression to that which is uncreated. Second, and this follows from the first dimension, the Catholic imagination is visual and embodied. It emphasizes seeing and is enacted in gesture, ritual, and performance. Third, the Catholic imagination stresses both the common good and the particular. While the individual is utterly important, he or she cannot be fully realized except in the context of community. At the same time the local, the particular, and the limited are of intense focus. Fourth, the Catholic imagination is paradoxical and ironic. It holds together impossible tensions of opposites. There is unity in diversity, hope within tragedy, and grace in the midst of grief. It is at the fine point of these tensions that I find Mary poised.[9] I will explore each of the aspects of the Catholic imagination from the perspective of Marian devotion. And because I have found that the most helpful theological reflection is done in the narrative mode or as a poetic enterprise, in each segment of my discussion I will include a story, an insight, or an image encountered along my Los Angeles pilgrimage road.[10]

SACRED TIME

On December 12, the feast of Our Lady of Guadalupe, the city of the Lady of the Angels, is awash in flowers. The festivities begin at dawn with *Las Mañanitas*, the "little morning" ritual in which *la virgenita*, the white dove, the rose, the beloved one, is wakened with tender songs. I doubt if there is a handful of the eighty-odd parishes in the archdiocese where this predawn ritual does not occur. Whether *las mañanitas* is attended by the "ethnic" community within a parish or, more likely, by just about everyone, the mariachi bands are strumming away, and toddlers dressed in girl-sized mantillas or tiny Juan Diego suits with penciled mustaches on their upper lips are draped over their parents' shoulders. During the daylight feast day hours, churches are alive with devotees who travel on their knees the length of the aisles toward centrally placed images of Guadalupe and her chosen one, Juan Diego, or sit quietly in pews breathing in her presence, or present her gifts and prayers. Lush bouquets of roses adorn formal altars as well as makeshift ones set up outside to accommodate the throngs that gather to add their own floral offerings, candles, and gifts to the profusion. Nor is it the day of the 12th alone that is observed: there are preparatory novenas (nine-day prayer rituals) and triduums (three-day observances) in many parishes and an annual archdiocesan torch procession the weekend closest to the feast that draws tens of thousands to East Los Angeles to participate: Aztec dance groups outperform each other, floats with girls dressed as *la Virgen Morena* drive by, the decades of the Rosary blare through loud speakers, confirmation classes parade, flags fly, bells peal, costumes are everywhere, and flowers, flowers, and more flowers are presented to her in every conceivable hallowed spot. Early December is sacred time in the Catholic Archdiocese of Los Angeles.

It is something of a truism in the academic study of religion that the religious imagination, no matter what the tradition, perceives that time is not uniform. There are instead sacred times during which a sacred sensibility prevails. Holy days and seasons, sabbath, Holi, and Ramadan, these are the stuff of a human religious sensibility that refuses to experience time as homogenized but instead as latticed with temporal windows through which the sacred reality at the heart of everything is glimpsed.[11] There is nothing unique about Catholicism in this, except that it might be said to have this sacramental sensibility in spades and to nuance this sensibility in its own fashion. Sacred times are not merely memorial in the Catholic way of things; they open out into eternity. Thus they are mediums through which the sacred power at the heart of all is available.

Of course the Roman Catholic Church has its own distinctive sacred calendar of times during which the central mysteries of faith are celebrated: the two focal seasons of the church year are Lent and the Easter season, during which the implication of the resurrection is explored, and the Advent and the Christmas seasons, during which believers plunge into the meaning of the incarnation. Jesus the Christ plays the premier role in this unfolding liturgical drama. The part played by Mary, his mother, is clearly a supporting one. Although the official Catholic liturgical calendar does provide access to the biblical story of the Virgin Mary as mother of Jesus and does set aside designated days on which her fuller dogmatic identity is celebrated—chiefly the feasts of the immaculate conception and the assumption—in the realm of popular devotion she commands enthusiastic allegiance and is much more prominent than the nods in her direction afforded by the universal church might suggest. It is also true that this tendency has been going on for a long time and that a countervailing tendency to restrict her to a secondary role that situates her more appropriately within the *kerygma* of the faith has also been ongoing.[12] Nevertheless, the Virgin Mary's presence in sacred time, whether she is recognized as Guadalupe or under another name, seems to spill over the confines of the normative Catholic temporal structuring and command a place in the popular imagination that is well beyond her role within the theological and liturgical confines of magisterial tradition. I do not mean to suggest that official recognition of the importance of popular devotion has been absent: December 12 is in fact indicated on the official Roman calendar, and the late Pope John Paul II, who was possessed of a strong Marian devotion, did raise *la Virgen Morena* to the status of empress of the Americas. But my pilgrimage to the minority majority city of the Lady of the Angels provides insight into the extent to which Catholic sacred time among large numbers of practitioners is distinctly Marian. It also gives insight into the power of these sacred times.

Guadalupe is not, of course, the only Virgin who commands the attention of her people at singular times in the Los Angeles archdiocese. The Filipino communities of the region have great devotion to their many miraculous virgins, especially Peñafrancia and Manaoag, and festivals among this community abound. In addition, on Wednesday nights throughout the archdiocese, novenas to Our Lady of Perpetual Help regularly draw hundreds of Filipino parishioners. These celebrations are matched by the Eastern Rite Catholic churches (those particular churches that follow the Byzantine liturgical rites but are in communion with Rome) that hold the August feast of the dormition of the Virgin dear. Thus, for example, in the village of El Segundo, just south of the Los Angeles airport, the Melkite and Russian Greek Catholic communities take to the streets on August 15 bearing the silver framed icon of the Mother of God depicting her "falling asleep" at the end of her life and her reception by her risen son. Similarly, on the vigil of Mother's Day in May, the various communities of Chinese Catholics converge at St Bridget's Chinese Center in historic downtown Chinatown for the festival of Our Lady of China, and on December 8 the archdiocese is alive with veneration of Vietnam's Our Lady of La Vang.

SACRED SPACE

In addition to sacred times, there are set aside sacred spaces created by and for the intense veneration that Mary's varied devotees feel. This too is typical of the religious imagination: shrines; sanctuaries; sites where founders walked or where ancestors dwell; places where healings are reputed to occur: Mecca; Jerusalem; the Ganges; Native American burial grounds; and other such sacred spaces are universally recognized. A sacramental imagination assumes that the visible world can be an expression of the invisible reality that sustains it. In the city of the Lady of the Angels, the architecture of sacred space is intensely Marian.

In the heart of East Los Angeles, hidden among a maze of one-way avenues and interrupted streets, is the Guadalupe Sanctuary. This exquisite jewel box of a church was founded in 1929 as a Mexican chapel, one of the small communities designated for Spanish-speaking Catholics. It has become a beehive of a site where nine weekend and two weekday masses plus additional services on holy days are celebrated and where individual and group prayer seems never to cease. The image of *la Virgen Morena* is everywhere visible in the sanctuary: above the altar she stands alone upon a sliver of a moon surrounded by the rays of the sun, her black belt of pregnancy visible beneath her prayer-folded hands. On either side of this central image are scenes from her story: the bird-song-announced encounter with the Aztec peasant-convert Juan Diego, his subsequent visits to the bishop to carry out the request of the beautiful lady dressed as an Aztec princess and declaring herself Mother of God, the bishops' rejection of his request for a shrine to be built in her honor, the sign of the roses in December that she produces, and the final conversion of the bishop as Juan Diego opens his rose-filled cloak to reveal the brilliant image of the Lady herself imprinted there. At this sacred site the central ritual action of the church, the Eucharist, is celebrated. But if one were not conversant with that fact, one might think that this was Guadalupe's church alone.

Nor is Guadalupe the sole Virgin to command her own spatial realm. Our Lady of the Rosary of Talpa, beloved patroness of Talpa de Allende in the Mexican state of Jalisco, has her own parish in East Los Angeles, as well as her own miraculous image and story (she is associated with a miracle of eternally burning candles). These are indelibly imprinted on the church structure itself: a monumental painting contributed by parishioners in 1944 and placed above eye level dominates one side of the church. In it Maria de Talpa, radiating

18

beams of light, is born aloft by a cascade of cherubs and angelic violinists while members of a donor family kneel devoutly on either side of the canvas. Across the sanctuary, seated upon her own pedestal, a porcelain-visaged version of Talpa carrying a pearled rosary, a tall cerulean crown cantilevered upon her sovereign head, and a silvery moon sliver beneath her feet, is venerated with freshly cut blooms. The same could be said of other titular Virgins of other parishes.

This is not a new phenomenon, nor is it restricted to ethnic images of Mary. Certainly, every church sanctuary has its designated Marian niche. Examples of Marian devotional patterns that dominated the Los Angeles Catholic landscape a generation ago also speak to the Catholic imaginative world in which sites are hallowed and experienced as places where one is ushered into the presence of the venerated figure, spaces where contact with the sacred itself takes place. I think of Immaculate Conception parish near downtown Los Angeles, with its utterly unique and glorious sanctuary windows completed in the mid-twentieth century, which depict Mary's varied reputed apparitions—at Lourdes, Knock, Fatima, La Salette, and so forth. Whatever one might think of apparitions (and this is a whole other topic), this sanctuary celebrates the imaginative possibility that in fact the material world is radically open to the realm of the divine. The two are not opposed but in intimate communication with one another. To hold up another classic example, scattered across the archdiocese is a striking series of black volcanic stone grottos replicating the 1858 appearance of the Virgin Mary to the peasant girl Bernadette Soubirous in the French Pyrenees, the site now of a healing pilgrimage shrine. The series was constructed by Ryoko Fuso Kado, a Japanese American Catholic who had been incarcerated in the internment camps during the Second World War and who vowed to construct a Lourdes shrine each year after he gained his freedom so that "people who pass by and stop to say a prayer may reach up their hearts to God in a much troubled world and thereby gain solace and consolation."[13] These grottos speak not only of a shameful historical event strangely transformed by artistic and spiritual generosity, but also of the power of the Catholic imagination to heal and redeem.

The point here is not only the rather obvious one that the Virgin Mary occupies large spatial and temporal swaths of the southern California landscape. Rather, it also is to suggest that layers of meaning accrue to times and places such as these. It is to suggest the depth of the religious imagination that would recognize the power of sacred time and space. Sacred time and space open out to the power and presence of the sacred itself. Not merely illustrative or pedagogical or memorial, such temporal and spatial sacramentality opens up the possibility of personal and communal transformation, healing, and renewal, all of which can be anticipated in the encounter with the sacred.

Scholars have approached this question of growth and change in devotional practices from a variety of academic disciplines. I will cite a few that help illuminate the phenomenon of Marian and other sorts of devotion and take us more deeply into the Catholic imagination. Using the tools of sociology, anthropology, and theological reflection, scholars such as Timothy Matovina, Gary Riebe-Estrella, and Thomas Tweed, among others, have explored the importance of popular devotion among exiled and immigrant communities and made sociological observations that help illuminate some of the extraordinary fervor associated with popular devotion and the way in which it can give rise to meaning. Tweed especially, through his study of the Miami shrine of *Nuestra Señora de la Caridad del Cobre*, has shown how the diasporic Cuban American community makes sense of itself as a displaced people. Tweed emphasizes the importance of the shrine in which narrative theologizing, institution building, and ritual practices express the transtemporal and translocative attachment of immigrants to their natal landscape and culture and script a dramatic narrative in which Our Lady of Charity becomes the leading mythic character. Other Marian incarnations like Guadalupe and La Vang are cherished by those who find themselves in an alien land or as part of marginalized or minority status groups.[14] The narratives and the rituals that occur in these sacred enclaves enable practitioners to negotiate the psychological and spiritual shoals against which life has battered them. Home, culture, and identity are all carried in the stories and rites practiced in the shrines and during the festivals of the Virgin patronesses of many nations and cultures.

Nor is it only recent immigrant Americans who carry with them the devotional imagination from their home countries as they transition to new, alien cultures. Pastoral theologian Mary Clark Moschella has written a fascinating monograph on the persistent habits of mind and heart among the second and third generation Italian and Portuguese community centered at Mary Star of the Sea, the large Catholic parish in San Pedro in the southern quadrant of the Los Angeles archdiocese. While many of these assimilated Americans may not be ardent churchgoers or engage in the overt devotional practices that their grandparents did, they nevertheless exhibit what Clark Moschella calls a "sacramental imagination" observed in the learned skills of visual and material piety that infuse the activities of daily life with a sense of the sacred, "a capacity for healing and creative transformation and situated values of connection, multiplicity and celebration."[15]

To push this Catholic sacramental imagination beyond its sociological and psychological dimen-

22

sions, it is good to be reminded that these sorts of Marian devotions make theological claims. To parse this Catholic way of imagining the world in a theological mode, one would say that it is a profoundly incarnational imagination. The hope around which the earliest Christians circled was that "God is with us." Just as Jesus fully human and fully divine was present with his disciples even after his crucifying death, the divine is present in the mystical body of the church, present in the eucharistic meal, present in the ongoing inspiration of the Spirit, and potentially present in all times and places. Thus, even as the divine and human, the ultimate and the passing, are not identical, one can know and experience something of the divine by being human. Incarnation is not simply a one-time event (although it is understood by the community to have had at one time a determinative effect). This intuition continues to play itself out across the span of centuries in a thousand ways.[16]

Another way of describing this imaginative approach, one that is sometimes highlighted in the spiritual traditions, is to say that the infinite is encountered only in and through the finite. This pushes the Catholic imagination in a *radically* incarnational direction. This insists that it is not simply that times and places are set aside to acknowledge the sacred reality or that the sacred might be encountered in time and space, but that

that sacred presence cannot be experienced *except* in and through the material, the temporal, and the concrete. To put it another way, to pursue the infinite, one does not leapfrog over real life. I have heard Jesuit Stephen Schlosser, referencing William Lynch, put it succinctly: the Catholic imagination has "faith in the ability of the finite to lead somewhere."[17] This also posits that the finite and the infinite are inseparably bound. There simply *is* no way to encounter God except through the created mediums, which include the heart, mind, and imagination of the human person. The theological anthropology that supports this vision is optimistic about the extent to which human beings are intrinsically God-directed or the extent to which they retain vestiges of the *imago dei* (image of God) in which humankind, as claimed in the first book of Genesis, was originally created.

This sense that the infinite and finite are tightly bound together is highlighted in the history and practice of Christianity, particularly in periods of Christian humanism, during which theology tended to be done "from below," beginning reflection with actual human experience rather than "from above," starting from abstract principals to work downward to humanity. The "renaissances" of the twelfth and sixteenth centuries and the era of Vatican II are examples of the ascendancy of Christian humanist perspectives in theology and spirituality. I think especially of the early modern

Ignatian (Jesuit), Vincentian, and Salesian traditions that celebrate human affectivity, intellect, and creative capacities as given by God for the full realization of humankind and for God's glory.

I mention this because it is not the only expression of the Christian or the Catholic imagination. The idea that it is *only* through the finite that the infinite is encountered has not always been assumed. University of Chicago philosopher David Tracy has famously described what he calls the analogical imagination, which he contrasts with a dialectical imagination, the former emphasizing the immanence of God, the latter the divine transcendence. He has suggested, and Andrew Greeley picks up on this thought, that in general the Roman Catholic imaginative world tends to be analogical while the Protestant imagination tends to be dialectical. One points in the direction of the sacred ground of being and posits what God is "like," while the other points by declaring what is "unlike" God. However, the dialectical imagination functions not only in magisterial Protestant traditions but within Catholicism as well. Tracy would see it as a necessary corrective to an excessive emphasis on immanence (one thinks here of the apophatic spiritual traditions of prayer or the emphasis on the transcendence of God found in the Rhineland or French school of spirituality); nevertheless, the analogical mode tends to be most characteristic of the Catholic imagination. While I think that Marian

devotion is preeminently an example of the analogical imagination, nevertheless, as I will argue later, a
dialectical sensibility is also implicit in the analogical and is discovered in Marian encounters: imagery
and analogical thinking at some point open out into
the mystery of unknowing, silence, and mystery.

AN EMBODIED AND
VISUAL IMAGINATION

The analogical is the imagination that undergirds the doctrine of the incarnation and the sacramental sensibility. It is the imagination that gives rise to the rich panoply of Marian devotional activities. Two assertions follow from this: the Catholic imagination is quintessentially a visual one and is fundamentally about embodied ritual; it is a performative, practiced faith. On any given day during the year, men and women, young and old, can be found in the still, dim interiors of Catholic parishes throughout the Los Angeles basin. They venture in alone or in small groups. They engage in scheduled novenas to Our Lady of Perpetual Help or reenact the Stations of the Cross. They rest quietly, heads bowed, or circle these sanctuaries, genuflecting before statues of Mary and the saints and touching their feet. They prostrate themselves and walk on their knees in gratitude, reparation, and adoration. They gather regularly for ritual actions and intone prayers in common. They turn the pages of devotional manuals and finger rosary beads. They pull small photographs out of jacket pockets and press them into the base of a *pietà* or an image of the Sorrowful Mother. They weep, sing, grieve, and seek blessings and forgiveness through private and collective gestures both small and expansive.

It is not that Catholics do not affirm certain propositions and adhere to creeds. But, despite recent emphasis on "litmus test" moral issues that are seen to define Catholic identity and that gain notoriety in the press, it is really ritual practices that historically and in the contemporary world both shape and reflect the Catholic imagination. Liturgist Bruce Morrill, medievalist Joanna Ziegler, and anthropologist Susan Rogers form a chorus to state it well: Catholicism is "fundamentally a faith of ritual practice, that is to say, a religion whose core theology, individual believers' inner spiritual experiences, and a great variety of social, communal identities come alive preeminently through participation in and ownership of rite."[18] The Eucharist is the primary example of this emphasis on ritual engagement, but the seemingly endless devotional actions, processions, rites of sanctification and coronation, ceremonies, and gestures that occur under the umbrella of Catholicism bear this assertion out. The Virgin Mary is the focus of a vast number of these rituals where she is both remembered and made present in the course of these different formal and informal embodied rites.

On a Wednesday evening in August, I make my way off the main streets of Glendale to an older residential neighborhood in which Holy Family parish is nestled. The sanctuary is open and with others I make my way inside to attend the weekly evening mass, which will be followed by a novena to Our Lady of Perpetual Help. The novena, a nine-day prayer cycle leading up to a liturgical feast or a weekly prayer done over a period of nine weeks, is a Catholic devotional ritual that gained currency in the nineteenth and early twentieth centuries and that has seen a resurgence in the Los Angeles area during the last twenty years. The vibrant Filipino Catholic community has been largely responsible for this devotional renewal. A variant, the one taking place at Holy Family, is a perpetual novena, in which one nine-week cycle is immediately followed by another. During the service, those of us gathered acknowledge Our Lady of Perpetual Help as maternal refuge, comfort in time of trial, and respondent to our petitions. Her distinctive Byzantine style image is set up on the front altar, and after the formal part of the service, devotees come forward to reverence her and offer their personal petitions.

Another one of the Filipino devotional celebrations that I witnessed in Los Angeles was the *Salubong*, which takes place early Easter dawn. Typically performative and dramatic, the central feature of the pageant involves two processions, one of men who carry a life-sized image of the risen Christ and one of women who bear a statue of his mother. For the duration of the lenten season the Marian image has worn a black veil. Now, as Easter morning dawns, the grieving mother is carried to meet her triumphant son: her black veil of sorrow is stripped away and replaced by a white veil of joy.[19] Then there is the block Rosary, a devotional practice that might have seemed moribund after the Second Vatican Council except that Vietnamese and Filipino Catholics have revived its practice. A statue of the Virgin is taken weekly to a new home where a group Rosary is prayed. She remains in the home for a week, at which time she is carried to a new home and the ritual repeated. Of course, a block Rosary builds community and cements cultural identity. But the imagination beneath this and other ritually embodied and visually oriented customs is much deeper. The gestures themselves and the visual imagery—statues, paintings, and such—are not merely depictions. They allow access to the reality they depict.

One of the things I have loved about my Los Angeles pilgrimage is being in churches that have their histories inscribed on their very walls. Liturgical architecture, of course, belies the era and theological sensibility alive when a building was erected, but it is the iconographical evidence left by shifting generations and cultural communities that is most expressive of the life of a parish over time. Immaculate Heart of Mary Church on Santa

Monica Boulevard just west of downtown, and St. Cecilia parish southward near the University of Southern California, are only two of the innumerable worship spaces that have the history of their congregations inscribed in the Marian images fashioned from stained glass, marble, plaster, metal, wood, and paint and enshrined in multiple, multilayered altars and alcoves. Immaculate Heart, established in 1910, was early on staffed by the Immaculate Heart Sisters, who had originally been brought from Spain to California in 1906 by Bishop Amat to fill the desperate need for teachers for the Catholic population in the frontier diocese. Devotion to the Immaculate Heart of Mary was a bourgeoning one in the early modern European Catholic world, a devotion shaped by the reforms of the previous centuries that had come to emphasize the Virgin as the model of virtue. Whereas in the medieval era she had been venerated primarily for her role as mother of Christ and bearer of the Word, now she was the example of the ideal Christian and of the emerging, more interiorized piety of the postReformation world. She was the one whose heart was to be extolled because of its obedience, humility, and submission. [20]

Another lecture would be needed to parse out the ecclesial, sociopolitical, and cultural implications of this immaculate hearted Mary for the sisters of her congregation, for women, and for humanity in general for whom she served as the model.[21] Suffice it to say that the statue that adorns the left front wall of the parish on busy Santa Monica Boulevard tells the story not only of those sisters' presence or the popularity of the devotion in the years between the seventeenth and early twentieth centuries, or of the spirituality promulgated in those years, but it speaks of the dominance of the Anglo-European congregants who long populated the area. The stained glass windows high on the side walls of Immaculate Heart come from a later era, when a forward looking pastor who was in residence during the late 1950s and 60s felt that all the ethnic communities then attending should be visually represented. Thus a modern looking version of Poland's Our Lady of Częstochowa looks down from her clerestory height on the right as one enters the sanctuary. More recent (postmillennial) layers of congregational identity are found in the removal from a crowded makeshift devotional shrine in the narthex to a prominent side altar of Our Lady of Peñafrancia, the miraculous Virgin from the Filipino Bicol Valley, and the subsequent erection of a handsome Guadalupe shrine in the next alcove. These new prominently displayed Marian images celebrate the dominant communities now active in the parish.

If the material world is the medium through which the immaterial is manifest, then it makes sense that seeing, the visual faculty, should be privileged in the Catholic scheme of things. After all, if you posit that "God is with us" and that this changes things, and if you claim, as does Catholic theological anthropology, that the divine image and likeness in which human beings were created has not been utterly effaced by sin but awaits cleansing, healing, or restoration, that is, sanctification, then that process ought to be visible. The saintly ones among us attract our attention; they draw us with their evident holiness; they "shine." They are sacred sites in themselves and draw us to the divine source by their light. Nor do they lose their power to communicate their light after their deaths. Certainly, they can be depicted. The panoply of statues and other visual images in Catholic churches and in common devotional use speak to this intuition. These visual depictions should not, however, be construed primarily as having pedagogical function: they *do* remind viewers of the history of faith and they *do* hold up exemplary models for imitation or admiration. They also *do* provide a sort of catechetical function and can appeal to those persons who may not have mastered literacy. But to dismiss visual imagery within the Catholic imagination as limited to these pedagogical or exemplary functions and to ignore the enormous power of visual piety is a grave mistake. Among those who study visual culture, David Freedberg, Colleen McDannell, and David Morgan have brought the complex impact of the visual to our attention.

It is no secret that the Catholic Christian landscape has for centuries been strewn with devotional images created by and for the believing population. Nor is it a secret that it is images that have most troubled detractors of devotion and that image making and veneration have been at the crux of ecclesial conflicts for as many centuries as visual images have been central to Christian experience. The perennial question that haunts Christianity is about the appropriateness of images to depict the divine. Although the *iconodules* (lovers and defenders of images) triumphed over the *iconoclasts* (opponents or destroyers of images) during the iconoclastic controversies of the seventh and eighth centuries, and although Roman Catholics of the early modern period reaffirmed (and reformed) the use of visual images in response to their Protestant critics, the issue has not gone away. Charges of inappropriate "worship" of Mary and the saints are still leveled against Catholics. In response to the question Do Catholics "worship" (the Latin is *latria*) images of the Virgin Mary? the answer is no. Worship belongs only to God. The technical theological understanding is that devotional images are venerated (*dulia*). Images of Mary even give rise to a separate technical term to describe the special honor afforded her: *hyperdulia*. Is this idolatry, as has sometimes been claimed? No again.

I have been aided in my own thinking about this by the above-mentioned scholars who have probed the issue of why human beings are in fact so drawn to images and are so affected by them. Religious images are in fact quite powerful and elicit striking human responses. David Freedberg was one early on who surveyed the past to consider the failure of art historians to deal with the abundant evidence for the ways in which people of all classes and cultures have responded to images, especially in emotional and psychological ways (as opposed to the critical or contextual approaches common in educated circles today). For, as he suggests, "people are sexually aroused by pictures and sculptures, they break pictures and sculptures, they mutilate them, and go on journeys to them; they are calmed by them, stirred by them, and incited to revolt. They give thanks by means of them, expect to be elevated by them, and are moved to the highest levels of empathy and fear."[22] These responses interest Freedberg, and he gives them their due, faulting our modern elite tendency to shy away from the power of images and their ability to evoke sensate and emotional response by retreating to critical or contextual analysis in their presence.

More recently, David Morgan has studied the ability of religious imagery to encourage interaction with believers who may wash, dress, address, study, incorporate them into their emotional lives, and reduce the aesthetic distance between an object and a believer. Morgan states it well when he describes the "lure" of religious images as being always bound up with the quest for something better, as having the capacity to allow people to see their way to new possibilities of self and community: "The lure of images resides not only in their promise of continuity or renewal but also of transformation. In every case, the lure answers to a deep longing, which it is the underlying business of religious belief to engage." [23] The act of looking itself, he proposes, is formative and constitutes a practice of belief. Morgan would identify looking, alongside thinking, wanting, deciding, and speaking, as well as ritual performance and gift giving, as part of the world-making activities that constitute social behavior. For him these are embodied forms of cognition and collective memory that reside in the concrete conditions of social life.

In a similar vein, Colleen McDannell continues the exploration of visual imagery from the perspective of cultural studies, identifying artifacts, art, architecture, and landscape as four bodies of evidence of a material culture that, she posits, is essential for understanding how religious people "anchor a worldview in the world." Studying religious worlds solely through ideas, or through the lives of persons seen as "strong," that is, not needing material representations of faith, privileges "spirit" over "matter" and in so doing gives priority to a strand of Christian orientation that sees icons as idols and assumes that untrained or "weak" persons might mistake the image of the divine for the divine itself. But in fact, the incarnational impulse is always present in Christian history and the image-making energy continues to assert itself. McDannell's explorations alert us to the possibility that we are perhaps rehearsing old arguments and falling into unconscious elitist modes of interpretation if we easily dismiss the importance of the visual and material dimension of faith.[24] The visual is certainly an axial aspect of the Catholic imagination.

Located just south of downtown Los Angeles, the imposing Lombard Romanesque-style Saint Cecilia Church contains many striking examples of the visual fecundity of Roman Catholicism and illustrates the way its history is visible on the community's structures. To the left of the main altar in this sanctuary erected in the 1930s is a Marian altar. The original fresco illustrating the 1858 appearance of Our Lady to the peasant girl Bernadette Soubirous at Lourdes, a seminal and representative focus of Marian devotion through much of the late nineteenth and early twentieth centuries, is found underneath a rather commonplace statue of Mary as Our Lady of Grace, her arms extended in gentle welcome. The altar below is crowded with devotional artifacts. To one side is a white-mantled Our Lady of Fatima statue, ubiquitous in the region during the 1950s at the height of the Cold War, when she was implored to save the world through the conversion of Russia, but not much in evidence any more.[25] In the very center, virtually obscuring the Lourdes fresco, is a glass cabinet containing an ornate image of *Nuestra Señora de Juaquila*, a devotion recently imported into the archdiocese by the *indios* from Oaxaca, Mexico, who venerate this small brown-skinned Virgin. A framed reproduction of the familiar Our Lady of Perpetual Help, an image originally promoted throughout the region in the early twentieth century through fiery preaching missions conducted by the Redemptorist order and recently revived by the Filipino communities, hangs on the wall to the left. Saint Cecilia is the home parish of any number of ethnic communities who are small in membership, including Nigerians, Guatemalans, and devotees of *Nuestra Señora de la Soledad* and *Nuestra Señora de Juaquila* who hail from regions of Oaxaca. Here they all find a home, each of these communities holding eucharistic celebrations and devotional rituals on varying Sundays during the month.

Religious imagery is central to the Catholic imagination as are ritual gestures, processions, and rites. As I have peregrinated the city of the Lady of the Angels, I have also had opportunity to encounter many of Mary's followers who honor her past appearances among the faithful and claim that she is present among us. The holy, as Greeley has said, "lurks" in creation. Objects, events, and persons are revelations of grace.[26] It is only a small logical step from there to positing visitations, visions, and apparitions. Help has come to me from several directions as I seek to understand this dimension of Marian veneration as an aspect of the Catholic imagination. First, U.S. religious historian Ann Matter has studied what she calls the "tabloid cult" of the Virgin and links its rise in America with cultural stress and contact with American Protestant fundamentalist rhetoric, which is suffused with apocalyptic end-time imagery. She sees Marian apparitions that predict dire events, especially apparitions that occurred after the 1917 Fatima appearances that took on antiCommunist political overtones, and similar recent visionary phenomena (that are not endorsed by the Catholic hierarchy) as embraced by those who exist at the fringes of American Catholic life. Janus-faced, on the one side these apocalyptic Marian devotees tend to face backward and idealize a type of devotion prominent before the Second Vatican Council and the ecclesial modernizing of John XXIII and Paul VI. On the other side they face fearfully forward in dreadful anticipation of the cataclysmic end-times. For many of these people, Mary stands at the head of the forces amassed against the principalities and powers.[27]

Not all Marian appearances draw on this sort of perspective, however. The classic example of a different sort of prophetic role that Mary might play is found in what Virgil Elizondo prefers to call the "encounter" with Guadalupe, an encounter that continues to heal, empower, enliven, and give hope to millions of her devotees. That she is experienced as having been and still being present among her people is undeniably true. What is it in the Catholic imagination that allows this? It is important to resist the immediate assumption that those who relate to appearances of the Virgin are simply uneducated or naïve. The crux of the question here again is an imaginative one, and concerns, if you will, the specific cosmo-vision that undergirds the conversations I have had.[28] Insight has come from two different academic directions from those who have fruitfully wrestled with the seemingly impassable disjuncture between the religious cosmo-vision of devotional piety and the more common worldview of modernity. Latino theologian Roberto Goizueta has targeted the modern post-Enlightenment-shaped cosmo-vision that diverges significantly from a pre-Enlightenment vision as one cause of a dismissive attitude toward popular religion. Goizueta, referencing the popular piety of Mexico, describes what he calls the "sacramental realism" implicit in the sorts of devotional practices I have been part of in Los

Angeles. He asserts that Mexican American popular religious practices embody an organic worldview in which the human person sees him- or herself as part of a relational network and a temporal continuum embracing all of reality, material and spiritual. This organic, holistic worldview, Goizueta claims, is at odds with postEnlightenment notions of time and space, of the material and the spiritual, and of the person's place within the material and spiritual dimensions of reality. Nonempirical reality is not dismissed as irrelevant but is factored into daily life through religious ritual and prayer. [29]

A very different perspective comes from Charlene Spretnak, who has made a bold statement about the sensibility around appearances and refuses to dismiss them. Spretnak describes herself as a feminist thinker and takes on both liberal feminism's critique of the Marian tradition and the fathers of the Second Vatican Council for "demoting" Mary to being mainly an exemplary model for members of the church. Her provocative *Missing Mary: The Queen of Heaven and her Re-Emergence in the Modern Church* instead reasserts the full spectrum of Mary's queenly and cosmic attributes as being upheld by recent postmodern physics and emerging scientific cosmology. She sees these traditional titles and attributes of the Madonna as corresponding to insights in the emerging scientific cosmology, especially contemporary reengagement with the cosmos as the fecund matrix or quantum plenum of all life. Spretnak critiques our modern perceptual orientation, which she feels has led to the demotion of Mary. She attempts to enthrone her once again with the help of postmodern cosmology. She writes, "One of the difficulties in understanding Mary's symbolic presence as the Maternal Matrix is modernity's atrophied ability to think symbolically with the subtlety and holism of religious consciousness in past times. The pre-modern mind had a subtle sense of religious symbols as being part of a larger, living context....Fortunately for our possibilities for recovery, the perception in postmodern science of an unbroken field of space-time as the nature of reality illuminates the pre-modern sense of religious symbols....the Creation is now understood to be a dynamic complex of relationships. The ground of one's being is the ground of the entire universe. Consequently, each entity exists not only in its local manifestation but also exists in relationship throughout the universe just as the entire relational universe exists in each entity....Mary is a gateway to our realization of that profound unity."[30]

Spretnak, Goizueta, Morgan, McDannell, and Freeberg, among others, have prompted me to probe my own unquestioned assumptions about the nature of time, space, visual imagery, and ritual practice and the way in which the Catholic imagination is shaped by and gives rise to the

Marian devotion I experience along my pilgrimage road. The ailing devotee who journeys in hope of healing to a Lourdes shrine, the person who lays flowers at the feet of Perpetual Help, or the one who tearfully entrusts a photo of a young enlisted serviceman or woman deployed in a war zone to the care of *la Virgen Morena* inhabits a perceptual world in which these actions are not superstitious but genuine encounter.

THE LIMITED, THE LOCAL, AND THE PARTICULAR

It is December 12 at Dolores Mission in East Los Angeles, the feast of Our Lady of Guadalupe. The mission structure itself is diminutive, and on a day as popular as this the pews are crowded. Pressed in between two family groups waiting for the service to begin, I find myself looking about at the blooms enveloping the Guadalupe shrine and the looped ribbons of green and red paper cutouts hanging from the rafters. There is, however, one odd item that I cannot explain: what looks like a lump of folded fabric placed on the low step before the altar. During the homily the Jesuit pastor identifies the mysterious object: these were the sole possessions of a young man found dead in the barrio just days before. Undocumented, he apparently had arrived from south of the border not long before in search of work. No one could identify him. Having no papers and no history here, he now had no name. Like so many impoverished and desperate young people, he had run afoul of someone or something in the gang- and drug-dominated neighborhood. The tiny bundle on display contains everything that was found with the body: a limp sweatshirt, a pair of worn jeans, scuffed sneakers. These items are placed before the altar in part to honor this boy, with his dreams and hopes common to any boy, and his dignity as a human being and thus a child of God. The pastor gives him the name Juan Diego because the Juan Diego of the Guadalupe story was, like him, a poor man, marginalized by the colonial society that had coopted his native lands and faith. The peasant Juan Diego was to all appearances a nobody, and yet the Guadalupe narrative puts him at the center of the story: despite his protests that the beautiful woman should choose someone else, someone of stature and influence to make her demands known, she chose him. He was her choice. The young man whose memory was held before us in the shape of the slight, folded,-fabric bundle, whose relatives from his native land will never probably know what happened to him, was for those of us gathered, Juan Diego. More importantly, it was understood in this troubled yet blessed barrio neighborhood where we gathered on this cool December morning, that we were the ones that the Virgin of Guadalupe holds up and calls her own.

A significant dimension of the Catholic imagination is the emphasis on littleness and particularity. Once again Jesuit literary scholar William Lynch says it neatly. "The heart of the human imagination, as of human life, must lie in the particular and the limited image or thing."[31] This emphasis plays itself out in a hundred ways in social and ecclesial life: the option for the poor, the moral principle of subsidiarity, a preference for the virtues and vows of simplicity, poverty and humility, a (guarded) tolerance for local cultural expressions of faith, a concern for the marginalized, the unborn, and the immigrant. This emphasis is in some tension with the equally strong instinct within the tradition for the common good and for common worship and defining statements of belief. Nevertheless, the local, the limited, and the particular have a special place in the Catholic imagination.

I find this strange and wonderful sensibility in the way that my conversation partners along my pilgrimage road speak about Mary and their relationship to her. On the one hand, while she is acknowledged by the vast majority of devotees to be a universal figure, she is intimately present to individuals and to very particular communities in ways that honor their distinctive identities. The Vietnamese know her as Our Lady of La Vang, who first appeared in 1798 deep in the jungle forests of Quang Tri Province and offered solace and healing to refugees fleeing from an intense persecution of imported foreign faiths and who has continued to protect her followers from suppression by competing feudal lords and hostile governments of all stripes. To Polish Catholics she is the Black Madonna of Częstochowa, who first came to them in the fourteenth century and later protected the famous monastery of the Bright Mount from the invading Swedes and more recently sustained them under Communist rule. Lebanese Maronite Catholics claim special intimacy with her because according to scripture, Jesus and his mother visited Lebanon during his public ministry. They venerate a sanctuary in the south of their home country dedicated to the Virgin at a place where Mary is believed to have stayed awaiting her son as he visited the cities of Tyre and Sidon. The local and the particular are recognized as cherished by the Virgin Mother, who spreads her sheltering mantle over those who turn to her.

This intimacy that devotees feel, this special regard that the Virgin bestows on them, are what I hear from my conversation partners all over the archdiocese. One evening I was invited to a weekly faith-sharing session held at the convent belonging to the Sisters of Notre Dame, a teaching order whose members operate schools with a particular mission of empowering young women. At the session, at which six or so of the community were present, I listened as these theologically updated, apostolically motivated women shared their stories of Mary in their lives. Some had come from pious family backgrounds and learned devotion at their mothers' knees, but all have an informed adult faith that includes Mary in some way or another. I was especially taken by one sister, a self-proclaimed "news junkie" and social activist who showed me her treasured modern version of the traditional image of Mary as mother of the church or mother of the faithful—Mary with her cloak spread wide to shelter those who gather underneath. This school administrator has named her image "Mary of the Folks," and she laughed when she admitted that it is to Mary of the Folks that she herself turns when a thousand times a day people come to her and hang on her skirts asking for favors and help of all kinds.

The scriptural Mary, of course, especially as she is depicted in the Gospel of Luke, proclaims the significance of the little, the lowly, and the poor. The much recited verses that the gospel writer has the socially insignificant, expectant young girl sing on her visit to her elderly, pregnant cousin Elizabeth, the *Magnificat*, is a rhapsodic song to the kingdom vision that would upend all unjust social arrangements and dignify those who are marginalized. Devotees of miraculous virgins and those who see in her appearances, or her "encounters," a sign that the lowly are chosen know this truth. The poor indigenous convert Juan Diego, the peasant girl Bernadette, the illiterate children at Fatima: these are Mary's chosen people, the ones to whom she inclines. As Virgil Elizondo has shown in his powerful vision of the role of Guadalupe in the lives of the people who claim her, the empowerment of those who are "the lowly" through the Marian symbol and the communal celebration of her patronage and protection is a reality.[32]

At the same Dolores Mission, where the small satchel of belongings from the anonymous young "Juan Diego" was honored, a distinctive painting of the Virgin hangs on the wall to the right of the main altar: *Santa Maria del Camino*. This unique image, the creation of Jesuit artist Fernando Arizti (the Jesuits have had pastoral responsibility for Dolores Mission since 1980), speaks of the significance of the little, the local, and the particular. Mary is depicted in a particular way as a young Latina with her serape-slung infant, walking barefoot along the road, with the skyline of downtown Los Angeles, seen from the perspective of the barrio of East Los Angeles, visible behind her. A striking detail is the surface of the road: ahead of her footsteps rough stones litter the path but behind, where she has walked, the way is smooth.

PARADOX AND IRONY

One of the most remarkable aspects of the Catholic imagination, and one that has seemed to be most elusive in practice, is its wonderful capacity to hold together irreconcilable opposites in paradoxical tension. Indeed, the entire Christian *kergyma* is centered on paradox: three in one, fully human-fully divine, life from death, an instrument of death as tree of life, virgin and mother. The paradoxes are not only doctrinal but play themselves out in the ecclesial life. I think Francis de Sales in the seventeenth century named it well when he coined the term *unidivers* or "unity in diversity." This of course is a difficult tension to realize in practice, and collapsing *unidivers* into rigid uniformity or letting it splinter into its diverse parts is always a delicate dance practiced, gracefully or not, on all levels of the church. How to be one body with many parts: that is the question.

Ever the polysemous symbol, in Los Angeles Mary has been in the past and is presently a figure who holds together impossible tensions within the ecclesial community. My pilgrimage encounters have borne this out. Most obviously, she has emerged in differing ethnic and cultural constituencies with a face and function that suits each group. For Los Angeles's Korean and Chinese Catholics whose originating cultures hold up progenitors and value progeny, Mary's motherhood is key. For the Benedictine monks at Vallyermo in the foothills of the San Gabriel Mountains, Mary is first and foremost the archetype of the contemplative, her ear and heart open to receive the divine Word. In celibacy and with ascetic rigor, these Benedictines look to the Virgin as model for their lives. For lay Third Order Carmelites, who wear her brown scapular as a sign that they are clothed in the garments of salvation and mantled with Mary's protection, she is an exemplar of the virtues of prayer offered in unison with the entire church and for all who do not pray. Armenian Catholics, fueled by raw memories of their own cultural genocide at the hands of Turkey, cherish her as Queen of Martyrs. Each Caribbean and each Latin American nation and many of their cities hold close their own miraculous image of the Virgin whose beloved story speaks of her preference and their particularity.

She adapts herself graciously to her locale and the aesthetic tastes of her local admirers. At Our Lady of the Valley in Canoga Park, she presides, fashioned in stained glass by the Piczek Studios, over the microcosm of the San Fernando Valley with its unique history and economy. In San Pedro

51

she looms above the busy harbor as Mary Star of the Sea, where she has been guiding sailors and fishermen into port since the earliest Italian and Portuguese seafaring immigrants settled there. In the beach town of Malibu she appears in a tasteful carved wood incarnation with flocks of sea gulls gathering at her feet. Mary holds all these disparate peoples under the shelter of her capacious cloak.

Even more remarkably, her welcoming arms extend broadly enough to embrace Los Angeles Catholics all along the ideological and theological spectrum. For many of her marginalized beloved, she creates an alternative world in which human dignity is not tied to economic or social standing. She embodies the promises of which she is heard to sing so eloquently in the Gospel of Luke. The lowly will be raised, the mighty cast down, mercies will reign from age to age. I have had Mary held up to me by progressive Catholics as just such a model of liberation, the one who sings of the end of injustice or the patriarchy; the mother who advocates for her disappeared and abused children and who is not afraid to confront the powerful and upend the status quo.

I have also had conversations with pastoral staff in the region who view her as protector of a world progressive Catholics might not recognize. A fierce defender of traditional piety and critic of secularism, this Mary is much beloved. I have spoken with those who promote the Militia of the Immaculata, a pious association founded by Fr. Maxmilian Kolbe, the Franciscan who died at Auschwitz. This association, which has roots in the de Montfort Marian Rosary revival of the eighteenth century, asks levels of commitment from its adherents that range from veneration of the Madonna to "enslavement" to being her "property" as she is seen to stand as a sacred bulwark against the secularization and decadence of the modern world. In a harmonizing if not identical key, I have also spoken with lay Catholics and pastoral volunteers who are devoted to a Mary whose final secrets hinted at during her appearances at Fatima have not, it is claimed, been revealed. (This despite a Vatican statement aimed at putting this speculation to rest.) The "third secret," I have been assured, issues an apocalyptic note and prophesies imminent collapse. This sort of Catholic Marian speculation is deeply shaped by the fundamentalist culture by which the American church is surrounded, speculation that has an apocalyptic edge. In this context Mary is warrior and boundary keeper par excellence.[33]

Most touchingly I have discovered places in which she has played the creative role of peace-maker. In a rather ordinary parish in Altadena, a wildly diverse community like so many in the archdiocese, where the inherent tensions among parishioners who on the streets are in conflict with one another—African Americans vs. Vietnamese vs. Mexicans vs. Filipinos vs. Koreans—a young pastor found that the one common ground these divided communities shared was their deep love of the Virgin Mary. An elaborate Marian congress was devised during which the disparate groups came together to pray multilingual rosaries, hear talks, and display their varying personal devotional images.

There is iconographical evidence of Mary's reconciling role throughout the archdiocese as well. Most prominent is sculptor Robert Graham's rendering of her at the new Cathedral of Our Lady of the Angels downtown. A youthful girl with racially unidentifiable features, she surmounts the majestic front entry doors, her bronze arms extended in welcome of all who enter. The cathedral's titular Lady of the Angels is not the only image created to represent the melding of cultures and ethnic identities that flourish in the minority majority metropolitan basin. There is, of course, the classic figure of Our Lady of Guadalupe, who, while she was not understood to have been created by an artist, is rightly identified by Latino theologian Virgil Elizondo as the "new creation." Elizondo makes much of the new culture that emerged from the encounter of cultures in Mexico. This unique culture is symbolized in Guadalupe herself, a *mestiza*, who is neither an Indian goddess nor a European Madonna; she is something new. He points out the iconographical significance of the visual image, the extent to which this particular *Virgen Morena* could be "read" by the Aztec people. The eyes, face, hands, the stars on her cloak, the sun in front of which she stands, the moon under her feet, the black band of pregnancy that girds her waist, the bird song and flowers in her tale: all these were symbols that spoke to the indigenous of a divine visitation, and of a new creation, a new harmony between peoples and cultures that gave hope to the natives (Juan Diegos all) who were both "most abandoned and most beloved." Guadalupe is for Elizondo the first truly American person and as such the mother of the generations to come who will synthesize the richness from their parent cultures and construct a society in which the barriers between peoples are broken.[34]

But in even more local and hidden iconographical ways than Guadalupe, Mary's reconciling capacity is evident. Our Lady of Peace parish in North Hills, another potentially fractious diverse community, after parish-wide deliberations, honored its titular Virgin by commissioning Los Angeles artist Lalo Garcia to create an outdoor fresco in which the Virgin's face might reflect the varied populations that the church served. The resulting Our Lady of Peace is once again a racially unidentifiable girl clothed in bright fabric upon whose upturned hands flutters a dove. She is the common ground upon which the diversity of worlds meets.[35]

An imagination that can hope for reconciliation and new possibilities even in the face of conflict and seemingly impossible stalemate is an enlivening one. I am reminded of the insights of Vie Thorgren, a contemporary interpreter of Vincentian spirituality (one of those early modern Catholic humanist spiritual schools), who contends that the Catholic imagination is "inventive to infinity." Referencing the pastoral practice of Vincent de Paul and Louis de Marillac, Thorgren points out that the central work of the Jubilee vision that the Gospel of Luke has Jesus proclaim at the beginning of his ministry (the passage that was Vincent's favorite) is the creation of relationships: relationships between the poor and the nonpoor, the outcast and the establishment. At the heart of Jubilee then are the creative possibilities that arise when all are invited to belong. The truth of humankind, in this Catholic imagination given Vincentian expression, is that under the fear and alienation that paralyzes and polarizes is the deep capacity for compassion and transformative friendship. A paradoxical imagination indeed.[36]

The Catholic imagination is of necessity an ironic one. Jesuit cultural historian Steven Schlosser has pointed out the deep irony in the Catholic imagination that permits both joy and tragedy. Its fundamental aesthetic moves from grief and loss of innocence to consolation, forgiveness, and redemption. God, he affirms, is found precisely in the ironic juxtaposition of hope and the experience of loss. Schlosser's research has identified this paradox particularly in the art and literature of the early twentieth-century jazz age Catholic revival, but the point can be more generally taken.[37] Everywhere in the diocese, Mary as Dolores, as Our Lady of Sorrows, is evident. At almost every turn on my pilgrimage road I have encountered her: eyes upturned and weeping, she cradles the body of her dead son in the iconic pietà. Shrouded in black she presses her hands together in unspeakable anguish; she swoons at the foot of the cross and bears her suffering in solitude. Nor are these representations of the sorrowful Mary merely images from the past, although many of them as artifacts are from an earlier era. But Mary's devotees migrate to these images. They bring offerings and flowers, *ex votos*, crumpled photographs of ones whose lives and flourishing hang by a slender thread.

These images point not merely to her solidarity with those who suffer nor to her consoling maternal presence but to the irony that even in the depths of sorrow the mystery of joy is incipient. There is nothing glib in this imagination, no pastel Hallmark card solicitude that masks anguish. Our Lady of Sorrows in Los Angeles carries in her heart the unbearable grief of countless losses that have been left at her feet. Mary, as she is experienced by her many followers, does not shy away from intimate encounter with individuals, nor does she turn her face from the suffering that goes largely ignored.

On the evening of Good Friday, I venture across the thin rivulet of the Los Angeles River once again to Dolores Mission, the Jesuit-run church community in the barrio of East Los Angeles. It has been difficult to determine if a *pesame* service is going to take place tonight or not. Dolores Mission has no staff person assigned to keeping up an informative Web page or to updating the parish voice mail. What happens there is mainly disseminated by word of mouth. Indeed, I discover that a community is gathered and already packed closely in the dimly lit interior—women, children, teens, men young and old, none exhibiting any signs of affluence or authority, and only a few Anglos like me. I mark once more the utter simplicity and functionality of the place. Up front in the tiny church, the altar has been removed and a life-sized polychrome statue of Dolores herself, the doleful Sorrowing Mother, stands in a pool of light, eyes upcast and hands clasped in anguished prayer, a large empty wooden cross and a presider's chair to her left. The event has begun: a recitation of the sorrowful mysteries of the Rosary, each in turn led by a different female member of the congregation interspersed with Spanish-language songs lamenting the unimaginable suffering of the mother as her heart is pierced by the death of her son.

Soon it is time for the young Jesuit pastor to seat himself in the presider's chair and begin his meditation on the weight of sorrow that Mary carries. The lights in the room are low, the air close, the mood of the crowd heavy. The priest draws us into the Virgin's grief with a first-person narrative crafted in the Ignatian imaginative meditation mode. "*Mi'ijo, mi'ijo*, (my son, my son)," he repeats soulfully. An antiquated projection screen unfurls from the ceiling above the mournful scene, and we view a brief emotive clip from a black and white European film featuring a wordless wild-eyed Madonna weeping as she clings to the foot of the cross under a stormy sky.

The meditation completed, sheets of paper and pencil stubs are passed, and we are invited to reflect on the burdens that weigh upon us. We inscribe them on our papers to present to the compassionate mother whose pondering heart alone can carry such grief. To the soft strumming of guitars we make our way up the center aisle, picking up carnations from baskets offered to us that we then lay tenderly at the feet of Dolores along with our intimate sufferings. The language of this service at Dolores Mission may not be my native tongue, the intense veneration, expressive emotionality, and the cultural inflection may be foreign, yet motherhood has led me here in my own idiosyncratic way, and I find myself at home.

As the *pesame* service concludes, community members are invited to share with the assembly what they have laid before the Sorrowing Virgin. The voices and faces of the women who now rise speak eloquently: "My boy has fallen in with bad men." "My daughter is very sick and dying." "I go to the prison to visit my son and I don't know if he will come home." "The drugs find our children even on the playground." Here there is no pain that is isolated, no sorrow that breaks the heart held alone, mine included. There is no grief so stinging that it is not already known and borne here in this humble shelter in the barrio of East Los Angeles, borne in the wisdom of those present and, most generously, by the Sorrowing Mother herself.

Mary does occupy a richly textured imaginative space in the wider Catholic imagination. She is at the center of sacred space and time, is guardian of the common good as well as of the marginalized, the local, and the powerless. She is visualized and honored by embodied rituals that usher the faithful into the sacred encounter that empowers, galvanizes, transforms, heals, comforts, and intuits joy in the midst of sorrow. To further explore this imaginative world, I turn now to that provocative phrase—*le point vierge*—that has continued to haunt me as I have traveled my pilgrimage road through the archdiocese under the sheltering protection of the Lady of the Angels.

MARY AS *LE POINT VIERGE*

The subtitle of this essay—*le point vierge*—I discovered first in the works of Thomas Merton, that ever-ready-to-explore-any-idea Trappist monk whose story and articulation of the monastic life so captured the imagination of the American public during the mid-twentieth century. Merton himself happened upon the provocative phrase in the writings of Islamic scholar Louis Massignon and immediately seized upon its poetic possibilities.[38] In his own turn, the older French scholar had been taken by the idea of *le point vierge* through his careful study of the tenth-century Sufi mystic of divine love, al-Hallaj, and continued to explore it after his own adult reconversion to the Roman Catholicism of his youth. So I follow the phrase back through this train of thinkers to the early medieval Islamic world. For al-Hallaj, the Sufi who was martyred for his more radical mystical statements, the *point vierge* was the secret place in the center of the human soul to which God alone has access. This virgin point, or as some have translated it, "virgin heart,"[39] was the goal of the Sufi mystical process of removing layers or veils from one's heart, a process accomplished through asceticism, meditation on the Qur'an, and acts of charity. The point of contact, beneath the seven layers of the heart, is *le point vierge*. Massignon for his part did Christianize the phrase and relate it to the long Marian tradition that viewed the Blessed Virgin as she was poised at the moment of the annunciation as humanity poised to receive the divine Word. But Massignon had a wider lens through which to interpret the phrase as well. Writing in the mid-twentieth century, and riffing on this central teaching of al-Hallaj, the French Islamicist saw the need for cultivating a virgin heart as a prerequisite for inter-faith encounter. What was needed, he believed, was a complete reversal of the attitudes toward other religions that were current at the time: what was essential was a radical hospitality in which the "Other" could be truly met. He specified that people get there by living according to *le point vierge*, that place of contact with God within each of us. Only when we live with and through the eyes of faith and love, which is what he means by living out of the virgin point, can we hope to understand the relationship of Christianity or Islam to God.[40]

From his cloister Thomas Merton carried on a lively correspondence with Louis Massignon. At some point, he became fascinated by the evocative phrase *le point vierge* and both spoke of it to his admired French correspondent and used it in his own writings. The ways Merton came to understand the phrase expanded its meaning. In one letter he referred to it as a sort of exhausted despair at the state of the world, the "virginal point, the center of the soul where despair corners the heart of the outsider."[41] This reading of the phrase is found in a series of 1960 missives to Massignon in which the Trappist reveals his anguish at the brutal violence evidenced in the French-Algerian conflict, an anguish shared by his correspondent. In another context but in a similar vein, Merton alludes to "the point vierge of the spirit, the center of our nothingness where, in apparent despair, one meets God—and is found completely in his mercy"[42] In yet another context the cloistered monk likened *le point vierge* to the temporal moment of passage from darkness to first daylight.

> The first chirps of the waking day birds mark the "point vierge" of the dawn under a sky as yet without real light, a moment of awe and inexpressible innocence when the Father in perfect silence opens their eyes. They begin to speak to Him, not with fluent song, but with an awakening question that is their dawn state, their state at the "point vierge." Their condition asks if it is time for them to "be." He answers "yes." Then, they one by one wake up and become birds. They manifest themselves as birds, beginning to sing. Presently they will be fully themselves, and will even fly.[43]

Perhaps even more significantly, Merton evoked the phrase in an account of his seminal contemplative experience—that "Fourth and Walnut Streets" event in Louisville—during which he awakened to the inner reality of ordinary passers-by who had never before claimed his attention.

> Then it was as if I suddenly saw the secret beauty of their hearts, the depths of their hearts where neither sin nor desire nor self-knowledge can reach, the core of their reality, the person that each one is in God's eyes....Again that expression, le point vierge (I cannot translate it), comes in here. At the center of our being is a point of nothingness, which is untouched by sin and by illusion, a point of pure truth, a point or spark which belongs entirely to God....This little point...is the pure glory of God in us....It is like a pure diamond, blazing with the invisible light of heaven. It is in everybody.[44]

Both a spiritual state, akin to the spark or apex of the soul to which the medieval Christian Rhineland mystics alluded, the location, as it were, of the ineffable encounter of human and divine from which all else has been emptied, as well as a state of created being where at the center of human nothingness one finds the Other, both the religious stranger and God, the virgin point seems to represent for Merton (as perhaps for the Sufi mystic and Massignon before him), liminality, the in-between-ness that returns us to the fresh possibility of re-creation as well as an apophatic experience that takes one to the very edge of the unsayable and unknowable. Mystical and political at one and the same time, the idea of *le point vierge* shimmers with numinous intensity.

I am aware that I run the risk of being grossly misunderstood in using the idea of the virgin point in my exploration of the figure of the Virgin Mary, even if I take it in a different direction than it may unfortunately often have been taken over the centuries in Catholic theology and spirituality. I am painfully aware that the concept of virginity, while a stunningly fruitful spiritual metaphor, has over the centuries been used oppressively to denigrate actual women and human sexuality in general. From the fifth century, when Augustine had to sort out the question of whether consecrated virgins who had been raped in the sack of Rome could still be considered qualified to claim their vowed state, to the centuries-long misogyny that stigmatized women as misbegotten males (who could overcome this only by overcoming their gendered identity), to the characterization of females as everything from "the devil's gateway" to the "weaker sex," to the dualism that has pitted Mary and Eve as symbols of good and bad females, to the persistent theological and pastoral denigration of marriage and sexual intimacy (identified with women), to the pervasive use of the Virgin to represent the sexless, obedient, good girl easily kept under control, to the "Marianismo" that extols the submissive, silent Latina who does not contest the machismo of her culture, the idea of Mary as Virgin has been sadly misused.

While I do not want to perpetuate these age-old sexist stereotypes and prejudices, I intend to be bold enough to hope that an expanded notion of the *point vierge* brought into conversation with the figure of the Virgin Mother may be enlivening and help us to think about her and ourselves in new ways.[45] For all she has led medieval armies and conquistadors into battle, for all she has served to shoo women religious back behind cloister walls, for as often as pious platitudes and vapid holy card images and narrowly conceived theologies may have imprisoned her, still I find a deep down freshness, a liberating energy in Mary. It was Jesuit literary interpreter William Lynch, once again, who asserted in an essay he wrote in the mid-twentieth century for *Thought* magazine that "the primary goal of human life is the liberation of the imagination."[46] At this point I'd like to take him up on his challenge.

In the first place, I have been struck as I have walked my pilgrim road, with the almost dizzying variety of Marys I have seen and met. These multitudinous identities seem not to trouble most of the people with whom I have spoken. Although I have been appropriately cautioned by Marianist

Fr. Johann Roten of the Marian Library at Dayton that all the Marys, whatever their visage or origin, must all remain identified with the scriptural Mary of Nazareth, and although Timothy Matovina has with compelling evidence claimed that devotion to Our Lady of Guadalupe cannot be described simply as an expression of Marian devotion, her role being too complex and her functions extending beyond those associated with Mary,[47] still I find her a central, powerful, and integrating symbol in the complex Catholic world. I have heard it said that Mary is such a rich, polyvalent, polyvocal symbol because of all the central symbols of Christianity, she is the least biblically well defined. That may be the case and that may provide her with sufficient flexibility to appeal to and respond to many different constituencies. Of course there are central Marian dogmas and a long tradition of Marian reflection, but these seem in practice simply to fold into the varied attributes and roles with which her faithful endow her. The tolerance for holding together in tension under one signifier—Mary—such a vast panoply of names, faces, qualities, capacities, and functions is a quintessentially Catholic one. In this sense, then, she is within the faith community a *point vierge*, a liminal, in between reality where the diverse hopes and aspirations of many converge: a space where out of darkness hints of daylight begin to emerge. I see in her the dynamic, creative potential of the collective Catholic imagination that, while continually refining and clarifying itself through structures and doctrines, also refuses to be reduced to those clarifications. Alive, in-breaking, generous, and unpredictable, Mary waltzes back and forth from the center to the periphery of the tradition and back again, choreographing a dance into which all are invited.

According to Massignon, who opened his Catholic heart to the Islamic vision, and according to Merton, who so openheartedly met all those folks at the corner of Fourth and Walnut in Louisville, *le point vierge* is the place where the Other is truly encountered. This certainly has been my own experience on the Los Angeles pilgrimage road. I suspect this idea first came to me when I visited Out Lady of Peace in North Hills and heard the story of the parish deliberations that resulted in the creation of the multiracial fresco of Mary that serves to remind parish members that the Christian work of reconciliation and peace-making begins in their intimate communities. My subsequent visit to Sacred Heart parish in Altadena, where the local Marian congress served to bring together constituencies that otherwise had little to do with one another, lingered with me. Mary as reconciling symbol not only expressed what people imaged and hoped for; she was also instrumental in bringing what was imagined into being. She became the mediating presence who facilitated an encounter with the strange and formidable Other. She became the common ground that enemies shared, the common ground of meeting and reconciliation.

Not only does Mary join communities of Others together, she has been at the virgin point of my own struggle to come into relationship with members of my own faith community who share little with me besides that affiliation. She has served as my own informal common ground undertaking. The polarized culture wars so painfully present in the American civil atmosphere are equally present in the American Catholic Church. I have found in Mary an entry point into the Catholic identity and the hearts of people on all ends of the ideological and theological spectrum. This has been important personal spiritual work. It has been good to seek to understand, to make sense of the motivations, the imaginative lenses, the anguish, and the hopes of those with whom I share a religious identity. It has also given me a glimpse of dawning, a new day, fresh with creativity and the possibility of renewed life.

But it is on another deeper level of encounter that in Los Angeles I discover Mary as the virgin point. There is something about the way my conversation partners describe their relationship to her, no matter what their perspectives on her or on life in general. There is a poignant tenderness, a palpable hopefulness that they communicate. There is no real reason why my interviewees should have been so forthcoming, so revealing of the depths of their love and longing in my presence except that their relationship to her is one of deep affection, and in me they recognized a similar love. They spoke not in a catechetical mode nor to impress or inform me but out of their deepest longing and most audacious hopes. Individual devotees may reject particular interpretations of Mary or be suspicious of other folks' way of perceiving her, but they all seem to have arrived at a suitable understanding that allows them access to an inner equanimity. She seems to represent, or even more provocatively to be present at, some deep, resilient space in the human heart in which newness and possibility germinate. I recall the voice of a sacristan in North Hollywood, a former actor whose near death experience from drug abuse brought him back to his childhood faith, and the serene gaze of another volunteer parish worker in Paramount as he assured me that if you look to Mary, she will lead the way to her son, and the joy of two members of a Rosary group in Pasadena who recounted the relational healing that had taken place in families because Mary cared, or the deep trust of the mothers of the barrios who entrust their vulnerable children to *la Virgen* and find in her compassionate presence the strength to survive.

Once more, the words of Thomas Merton come to mind. Writing of contemplative prayer, his words capture something of my sense of this profound *point vierge* that I have sensed in the hearts of those who share their words about Mary with me. It is here that the analogical imagination opens out into the apophatic experience.

> In the "prayer of the heart" we seek first of all the deepest ground of our identity in God. We do not reason about dogmas of faith, or "the mysteries." We seek rather to gain a direct existential grasp, a personal experience of the deepest truths of life and faith, finding ourselves in God's truth....[48]

Beneath the veils that cover the heart, beneath our fears and views and ego-driven ideologies is a space, a virgin space not in the sense of absence of ambiguity nor pure because it denies the vagaries of the human heart with its cruel and destructive capabilities, but a space so deep and so poised at the edge of unknowing and the unsayable, that the outer layers that cover the heart are peeled away and yield to silence. A point where the stranger is encountered in the full mystery of otherness. A point where tensions meet and, not resolved, still create new possibilities. A threshold where the ultimate divine Other invites. At this point the heart breaks open and what remains is mercy, grace, forgiveness, reconciliation, hope, and beauty, beauty, and more beauty.[49]

NOTES

1. The as yet unpublished manuscript that has emerged from this project is presently entitled *The Lady of the Angels and Her City: A Marian Pilgrimage*. Several of the stories from that manuscript have been adapted for this essay.

2. My chief and indispensable guides on this pilgrimage were Dr. Michael Downey, Cardinal Mahony's theologian, and Fr. Michael Engh, SJ, historian of religious Los Angeles and presently president of Santa Clara University.

3. Names suggested as original include the City of Our Lady of the Angels, the City of Our Lady of the Angels of the River Porciuncula, the City of Our Lady of the Angels of the Porciuncula, or the City of the Queen of the Angels. Perhaps the most trustworthy possibility is *El Pueblo de Nuestra Señora de los Angeles del Rio Porciúncula* (the town of Our Lady of the Angels on the Porciuncula River). On the conflict about the city name, see the *Los Angeles Times* story by Bob Pool, "City of Angels' First Name Still Bedevils Historians," March 26, 2006.

4. These include Elizabeth A. Johnson, *Truly Our Sister: A Theology of Mary in the Communion of Saints* (New York: Continuum, 2003); Sally Cunneen, *In Search of Mary: The Woman and the Symbol* (New York:

Ballantine Books, 1997); George H. Tavard, *The Thousand Faces of the Virgin Mary* (Collegeville, MN: Liturgical Press, 1996); Linda B. Hall, *Mary, Mother and Warrior: The Virgin in Spain and the Americas* (Austin: University of Texas Press, 2004); Ann E. Matter, "Apparitions of the Virgin Mary in the Late Twentieth Century: Apocalyptic, Representation, Politics," *Religion* 31:125–53; Sandra L. Zimdars-Swartz, *Encountering Mary: From La Salette to Medjugorje* (Princeton: Princeton University Press, 1991); William Christian Jr., *Apparitions in Late Medieval and Renaissance Spain* (Princeton, NJ: Princeton University, Press, 1989); and his *Visionaries: The Spanish Republic and the Reign of Christ* (Berkeley, CA: University of California Press, 1996); Chris Maunder, "Apparitions of Mary," in *Mary: The Complete Resource*, ed. Sarah Jane Boss (Oxford: Oxford University Press, 2007): 424–57. A useful resource for recent magisterial statements about the Virgin Mary is *Mary in the Church: A Selection of Teaching Documents* (Washington, DC: USCCB Publishing, 2003). It includes the 1973 statement by the U.S. Bishops, Pope Paul VI's 1974 exhortation, Pope John Paul II's 1987 encyclical, and his 2002 apostolic letter. See also *Lumen Gentium*, Dogmatic Constitution on the Church, from the Second Vatican Council, chap. VIII.

5. The project of academic study of spirituality is described in several recent publications, including Sandra M. Schneiders, "Approaches to the Study of Christian Spirituality," in *The Blackwell Companion to Christian Spirituality*, ed. Arthur Holder (Oxford/Malden, MA: Blackwell Publishing, 2005), 15–33; *Minding the Spirit: The Study of Christian Spirituality*, ed. Elizabeth A.

Dreyer and Mark S. Burrows (Baltimore/London: Johns Hopkins University Press, 2005); *Exploring Christian Spirituality: Essays in Honor of Sandra M Schneiders, IHM*, ed. Bruce H. Lescher and Elizabeth Liebert, SNJM (New York/Mahwah, NJ: Paulist Press, 2006). *Spiritus: The Journal of the Society for the Study of Christian Spirituality* represents the cutting-edge work in the field.

6. The following scholars have ably explored the topic and I draw upon their insights. William F. Lynch, SJ, *Images of Hope: Imagination as Healer of the Hopeless* (Helicon, 1965), and *Images of Faith: An Exploration of the Ironic Imagination* (University of Notre Dame Press, 1973); David Tracy, *The Analogical Imagination: Christian Theology and the Culture of Pluralism* (NY: Crossroad, 1981); Gerald J. Bednar, *Faith as Imagination: The Contribution of William F. Lynch, SJ* (New York: Sheed and Ward, 1996); Andrew Greeley, *The Catholic Imagination* (Berkeley: University of California Press, 2000); Stephen Schlosser, SJ, *Jazz Age Catholicism: Mystic Modernism in Postwar Paris, 1919–1933* (Toronto: University of Toronto Press, 2005).

7. Mary Warnock, *Imagination* (Berkeley: University of California Press, 1976).

8. William F. Lynch, SJ, "Theology and the Imagination," *Thought* 29 (Spring 1954): 76.

9. I have not mentioned all of the dimensions of the Catholic imagination that other scholars have pointed out. Notably, Greeley lists hierarchy, the mother love of God, sacred desire, and socialization as aspects that I have not chosen to flesh out here.

10. Andrew Greeley and Christopher Pramuk, better than I, have emphasized the wisdom of narrative or

"sapiential" theological discourse. See Greeley's *The Catholic Imagination* and Pramuk's *Sophia: The Hidden Christ of Thomas Merton* (Collegeville, MN: Liturgical Press, 2009).

11. The older truism hallowed in the classic literature of religious studies, that the sacred and the profane are diametrically opposed in the religious imagination, has been challenged by scholars of material culture like Colleen McDannell, who points out that that imagination sees traces of the sacred in all dimensions of the "ordinary" and "profane" world. See her *Material Christianity: Religion and Popular Culture in America* (New Haven: Yale University Press, 1995).

12. Notable moments during which Marian devotion and Mariology have been downplayed or reformed were the early modern period of the Catholic Reformation and the Second Vatican Council. A recent statement about the role of "devotion" and magisterial distinctions between that and "popular piety" is found in Congregation for Divine Worship and the Discipline of the Sacraments, *Directory on Popular Piety and the Liturgy: Principles and Guidelines* (Vatican City: 2001), nos. 7–10.

13. On Ryoko Fuso Kado consult *Encyclopedia of California's Catholic Heritage*, 427.

14. *Horizons of the Sacred: Mexican Traditions in U.S. Catholicism*, ed. Timothy Matovina and Gary Riebe-Estrella (Ithaca: Cornell University Press, 2002); Thomas A. Tweed, *Our Lady of the Exile: Diasporic Religion at a Cuban Catholic Shrine in Miami* (New York/Oxford: Oxford University Press, 1997).

15. Mary Clark Moschella, *Living Devotions: Reflections on Immigration, Identity and Religious*

Imagination (Eugene, OR: Pickwick Publications, 2008).

16. For example, that great saint of the medieval era, Francis of Assisi, was one who performed the Christian life. His shockingly theatrical and embodied spirituality—ripping his clothes off in the public square as he enacted his "new birth" as the son of the heavenly father, celebrating the joy of being forgotten and cast out as radical identification with the God who came naked into the world and left it naked and abandoned on a cross—this was the incarnational imagination acted out upon the public stage of his time. Lawrence Cunningham has beautifully brought this performing dimension of Francis' witness to life in his *Francis of Assisi: Performing the Gospel Life* (Grand Rapids, MI: Eerdmans, 2004).

17. Stephen Schlosser, SJ, lecture, "Holy the Firm: Irony, Hope, and Catholic Imagination," given on November 11, 1997, at Creighton University.

18. *Practicing Catholic: Ritual, Body and Contestation in Catholic Faith*, ed. Bruce T. Morrill, Joanna E. Ziegler, and Susan Rogers (New York: Palgrave Macmillan, 2006), 3.

19. This custom, popular in the Philippines, has its germ in the meditation on Mary's encounter with her risen son brought to the islands by Jesuit missionaries. Ignatius Loyola in his *Spiritual Exercises*, which all his spiritual heirs undergo, imagined this joyful family encounter.

20. On early modern changes in the Virgin's image, see Donna Spivey Ellington, *From Sacred Body to Angelic Soul: Understanding Mary in Late Medieval and Early Modern Europe* (Washington, DC: Catholic

University of America Press, 2001). The evolution of the IHM congregation and its spirituality is another fascinating story. See Anita Caspary, *Witness to Integrity: The Crisis of the Immaculate Heart Community in California* (Collegeville, MN: Liturgical Press, 2003).

21. I have made an attempt to decode this Mary in an article focused on the early modern Salesian tradition. See Wendy M. Wright, "The Ambiguously Gendered Ideal of a Seventeenth-Century Community of Women Religious: The Visitation of Holy Mary," ed. Susan Calef and Ronald Simkins, *Journal of Religion and Society* 11, supplement series 5 (2009): 103–13. Available at http://moses.creighton.edu/JRS/2009/2009-14.html.

22. David Freedberg, *The Power of Images: Studies in the History and Theory of Response* (Chicago: University of Chicago Press, 1989).

23. David Morgan, *The Lure of Images: A History of Religion and Visual Media in America* (Routledge, 2007), 261–62.

24. See Colleen McDannell, *Material Christianity*.

25. Fatima does remain a focal point of devotion among the Vietnamese community and among some traditionalist Catholics. And she is still the central image of Mary promoted by the Blue Army. For an article on this organization at the time of Vatican II, see Harold Colgon, "The Blue Army of Our Lady," *The Marian Era: World Annual of the Queen of the Universe*, vol. 6 (Franciscan Herald Press, 1965), 24–49, 98.

26. Andrew Greeley, *The Catholic Imagination* (Berkeley: University of California Press, 2000), 1.

27. Ann E. Matter, "Apparitions of the Virgin Mary in the Late Twentieth Century: Apocalyptic, Representation,

Politics," *Religion* 31:125–53. See also Sandra L. Zimdars-Swartz, *Encountering Mary: From La Salette to Medjugorje* (Princeton: Princeton University Press, 1991).

28. I first encountered the term *cosmo-vision* in Michael Amaladoss, SJ, "Toward a New Ecumenism," in *Popular Catholicism in a World Church: Seven Studies in Inculturation*, ed. Thomas Bamat and Jean-Paul Wiest (Maryknoll, NY: Orbis Books, 1999), 272–301.

29. Roberto S. Goizueta, "Making Christ Credible: U.S. Latino/A Popular Catholicism and the Liberating Nearness of God," in *Practicing Catholic,* 169–78. See also his "The Symbolic World of Mexican American Religion," in *Horizons of the Sacred*, 119–37. These quotes are from pp. 123–25.

30. Charlene Spretnak, *Missing Mary: The Queen of Heaven and Her Re-Emergence in the Modern Church* (New York: Macmillan Palgrave, 2004):101–5.

31. William Lynch, SJ, *Thought* 33 (Summer 1958): 206.

32. Virgil Elizondo, *Guadalupe: Mother of the New Creation* (Maryknoll, NY: Orbis Books, 1997).

33. This is not, of course, the first instance in which Mary has served as a warrior presence. She was this par excellence in the fifteenth-century *Reconquista*, during the colonial expansion into the New World, in the early modern Catholic Reformation, during the nineteenth century, and so forth. See especially Linda Hall, *Mary, Mother and Warrior*.

34. Elizondo, *Guadalupe*, esp. 100–112.

35. The attempt to create Marian images that reconcile diverse Catholic communities is not brand new.

An article from *The Tidings*, the Los Angeles arch-diocesan newspaper, dated March 5, 1955, describes a Marian statue carved "from many woods" on display at St Mary's College, each wood coming from a part of the globe where Catholicism is planted.

36. Vie Thorgren, "Inventive to Infinity," unpublished lecture given at Creighton University, September 2000.

37. Stephen Schlosser, SJ, *Jazz Age Catholicism*.

38. Merton was undoubtedly familiar with the traditional Marian resonance of the term as was Massignon, but it seems to have struck him anew in the context of the correspondence, which dealt with political and social issues as well as with Sufism.

39. Dorothy C. Buck translates the phrase this way. See her "The Theme of *Le Point Vierge* in the Writings of Louis Massignon." Available http://www.dcbuck.com/Talks/Massignon.html.

40. The most thorough article on Merton and Massignon and *le point vierge* is by Sidney H. Griffith, "Thomas Merton, Louis Massignon and the Challenge of Islam," *The Merton Annual*, vol. 3 (1990): 151–73. I am indebted to Christian Krokus for his helpful explanation of *le point vierge* in the writings of Massignon.

41. Thomas Merton, *Witness to Freedom: The Letters of Thomas Merton in Times of Crisis*, ed. William H. Shannon (New York: Farrar Straus Giroux, 1989), 278.

42. Thomas Merton, *Conjectures of a Guilty Bystander* (New York: Doubleday, 1968), 151.

43. Ibid., 131.

44. Ibid., 156.

45. I hope I do this in concert with a number of other feminist scholars who could well be said to be engaged in writing Third Wave Mariology. Sarah Jane Boss in Wales and Tina Beattie in England as well as Aurelie Hagstrom and Charlene Spretnak here in the United States—each approaches the topic of Mary from divergent perspectives, but they all take up traditional titles and attributes applied to the Virgin and turn them in new directions.

46. Lynch, "Theology and the Imagination," 76.

47. Matovina describes the symbol of Guadalupe at San Fernando Mission as encompassing patriotism; political protest; divine retribution and covenant renewal; ethnic solidarity and reinforcement of social hierarchy; a model of feminine virginity and domesticity and an inspiration for women to be active in the public arena and demand equality; a plea for miraculous intervention; and an inducement for greater participation in the church's sacramental life. She "...also provided a ritual arena for Mexicans and Mexican-Americans to forge and celebrate an alternative world, one in which powerful realities like exile and racism could be defined and re-imagined. A brown skinned 'exile' herself Guadalupe was a treasured companion whose faithful encountered her most intensely in the midst of the displacement discrimination, degradation, and all the difficulties they endured." See Timothy Matovina, *Guadalupe and Her Faithful: Latino Catholics in San Antonio from Colonial Origins to the Present* (Baltimore: Johns Hopkins University Press, 2005).

48. Thomas Merton, *Contemplative Prayer* (New York: Image Books, 1996), 67.

49. Of course Mary has long held the title *tota pulchra*, the all beautiful. On this see the excellent article by Johann G. Roten, SM, "Mary and the Way of Beauty," *Marian Studies* XLIX (1998): 109–27. Even in this article, however, and certainly in magisterial statements, I find that the language of beauty—she is "the all beautiful creature, the mirror without stain, the supreme ideal of perfection"—tends to be rather static and locked into a European aesthetic. It feels somehow overly concerned with docility, purity, and correctness. The experience of the rich cultural diversity in Los Angeles and the living presence of Mary in those communities open up the experience of beauty. The imaginative language of beauty, visual and linguistic, here seems to me to "sing." It feels expansive, passionate, prophetic, and complicated, and thus true to experience.

The Madeleva Lecture in Spirituality

This series, sponsored by the Center for Spirituality, Saint Mary's College, Notre Dame, Indiana, honors annually the woman who as president of the college inaugurated its pioneering graduate program in theology, Sister M. Madeleva, C.S.C.

1985
Monika K. Hellwig
Christian Women in a Troubled World

1986
Sandra M. Schneiders
Women and the Word

1987
Mary Collins
Women at Prayer

1988
Maria Harris
Women and Teaching

1989
Elizabeth Dreyer
Passionate Women: Two Medieval Mystics

1990
Joan Chittister, OSB
Job's Daughters

1991
Dolores R. Leckey
Women and Creativity

1992
Lisa Sowle Cahill
Women and Sexuality

1993
Elizabeth A. Johnson
Women, Earth, and Creator Spirit

1994
Gail Porter Mandell
Madeleva: One Woman's Life

1995
Diana L. Hayes
Hagar's Daughters

1996
Jeanette Rodriguez
Stories We Live
Cuentos Que Vivimos

1997
Mary C. Boys
Jewish-Christian Dialogue

1998
Kathleen Norris
The Quotidian Mysteries

1999
Denise Lardner Carmody
An Ideal Church: A Meditation

2000
Sandra M. Schneiders
With Oil in Their Lamps

2001
Mary Catherine Hilkert
Speaking with Authority

2002
Margaret A. Farley
Compassionate Respect

2003
Sidney Callahan
Women Who Hear Voices

2004
Mary Ann Hinsdale, IHM
Women Shaping Theology

[No Lecture in 2005]

2006
Susan A. Ross
For the Beauty of the Earth

2007
M. Shawn Copeland
The Subversive Power of Love

2008
Barbara Fiand
Awe-Filled Wonder